D1212718

100

DVD CONTENTS

The Open Road Tour

The exhibits, music and other activities from all of the sites of
The Open Road Tour.

The Ride Home

A journey with the riders as they traveled home to Milwaukee.

The Celebration

The three day celebration in Milwaukee.

The Parade

Highlights from the parade as 10,000 bikes traveled through the
streets of Milwaukee.

The Party

Live footage of the Sunday event featuring the music, the people,
the fireworks and the birthday ceremony that kicked off another
century of great motorcycles.

Rider Gallery

A montage of photographic moments highlighting the people and
the events that made up the 100th Anniversary celebration.

THE HARLEY-DAVIDSON 100TH ANNIVERSARY
RETROSPECTIVE BOOK & DVD

Harley-Davidson Motor Company

100th Anniversary Executive Producer: Robert Butters
Book Design: Abbott Miller and Jeremy Hoffman, Pentagram
Editor: Ileen Gallagher
DVD Production: @ radical.media
Book Production: World Online Merchandising

Copyright © 2003 H-D, All rights reserved

No part of this book may be reproduced in any form or by
any electronic or mechanical means, including information
storage and retrieval systems, without express written
permission of Harley-Davidson Motor Company.

Harley-Davidson, Harley Owners Group, H.O.G., the bar and
shield logo, MotorClothes, Buell, Lightning, Blast, Sportster,
and the 100th Anniversary logo are among the trademarks
of H-D Michigan Inc. All other trademarks are the property
of their respective owners.

First Edition
ISBN 0-9746185-0-0

Printed, manufactured, and bound in the United States
of America

Principal photography: Peter Turnley, Victor Fisher,
Andrew Rosenthal, Michael Lewis, David Turnley

Exhibition photography: John R. Glembin, Timothy
Hursley, Harry Zernike

Additional photography: Bobbie Buchholz, Brad
Chaney, Terry Haller, John R. Glembin, Nathan B.
Harrmann, Dave Kotlan, Kelly Riolo, Theresa Schauer,
Crystal Sokoloff, Dale Stenton, Mike Zimmerman,
T. Zumpano

CONTENTS

Foreword   8

The Open Road Tour   10

The Harley-Davidson Experience   32

Muscular Dystrophy Association   56

Musical Performances   60

Stunt and Drill   72

The Ride Home   78

The Celebration   90

The Parade   102

The Party   108

FOREWORD

On August 31, 2003, an estimated 150,000 riders and enthusiasts gathered in Milwaukee, Wisconsin, on the shores of Lake Michigan, to celebrate the 100th anniversary of Harley-Davidson.

This book, and the accompanying DVD, are a look back at the events which took place during the 14 months of celebrating this once-in-a-lifetime event.

When the three Davidson brothers and Bill Harley joined together in 1903 to build motorcycles, they never could have imagined what would follow.

In a journey spanning 100 years, the Motor Company has seen its responsiveness tested during the world wars; its commitment to never compromise threatened during the AMF years, and its survival skills tested in the early eighties. Ultimately, it has emerged from a remarkable turnaround with extraordinary growth.

To say that there was a lot to celebrate is an understatement.

Yet everyone involved knew that if the Harley-Davidson 100th Anniversary celebration was going to be memorable, it was going to have to be big and it was going to have to reach across the globe. It was going to have to bring the party to the people by staging an event so ambitious, that before it was through it would span 14 months, involve nine cities, four continents, and travel 32,500 miles. Like never before, The Open Road Tour would pay tribute to the Journey, the Culture, the Machine, and the Ride.

And then the celebration would come home. With riders from around the world, leaving from Washington D.C., Portland, Oregon, Baton Rouge, Louisiana and Las Vegas, Nevada all converging for the final four days of events in Milwaukee.

For those who found a way to be part of it, the 100th anniversary was an event that will be remembered forever. For those who may have sat on a Harley-Davidson® motorcycle for the first time, and understood what all the passion is about, welcome to the family.

THE OPEN ROAD TOUR

It started in July of 2002, and by the time the last exhibit was taken down in Hamburg in July 2003, and everything was packed away, The Open Road Tour stood as testament to 100 years of great motorcycles and their ability to transcend cultures throughout the world.

When the Harley-Davidson Open Road Tour opened at its first venue in Atlanta, Georgia, it consisted of 80,000 square feet of exhibits in four main tents, top musical entertainment, stunt riders, drill teams, movies, activities for kids, fashion shows, and of course motorcycle demo rides.

The logistics were staggering. For example, all of the bikes and one-of-a-kind artifacts on loan from the Harley-Davidson Archives, including the 1956 K Model once owned by Elvis Presley, traveled by air on chartered jets in a secure, climate-controlled environment. By land, over 90 semi-trailers were required to transport the show, which equated to 40 sea containers when needed to cross the oceans.

Milwaukee
August 28–31, 2003

Toronto
September 28–29, 2002

Barcelona
June 27–29, 2003

Los Angeles
September 6–8, 2002

Dallas
October 26–27, 2002

Baltimore
August 16–18, 2002

Atlanta
July 19–21, 2002

The Open Road Tour

Hamburg
July 25-27, 2003

7 **Tokyo**
April 26-27, 2003

6 **Sydney**
March 14-16, 2003

Open Road Tour Build

When The Open Road Tour arrived at a new venue, it took three days just to unload everything. And then it all had to be put together. There were four massive 20,000 square foot tents to be erected, which served as home for the exhibits in the domestic venues. Over 100 beam-rigging clamps were used in each exhibit tent, from which thousands of lights and exhibit sections were hung.

Internationally, The Open Road Tour exhibits were housed indoors with each location requiring specific build considerations. For example, a 65-foot high dome structure in Sydney marked the first time all of the exhibits were housed under one roof. Weeks later, a custom structure was built for Barcelona in order to house portions of the exhibit the main building could not contain.

In Atlanta, setting up The Open Road Tour took three weeks. In Hamburg, it took five days. At every location, an estimated 690,000 watts of electricity were used during the event. That's enough energy to power a small city for a day.

Open Road Tour
Sites

There was a method to the madness. A site had to have a minimum area of 40 acres, with access to and from major freeways. It had to have parking for 10,000 bikes. It had to be available for three weeks to allow for the set up. And it had to be in a place where thousands of riders would be made to feel welcome.

It also had to fit into the bigger scheme of things so that collectively the venues were geographically disbursed, putting the greatest number of people within riding distance.

International site selection was equally focused on the logistics of staging a large event, but in a departure from the domestic venues, the emphasis was on allowing the flavor of each particular city to become part of the event.

⭐ Atlanta

Atlanta Motor Speedway

July 19–21, 2002

Combining the event with the 19th Annual H.O.G.® Rally, the Atlanta Motor Speedway served as the inaugural site for The Open Road Tour. Thousands of riders and H.O.G. members from across the country participated in the event and braved temperatures that climbed above 110 degrees as a heat wave gripped the region.

 **Baltimore**

Pimlico Race Track

August 16–18, 2002

It was a case of horses meeting horsepower when the Pimlico Race Track, home to the Preakness, hosted The Open Road Tour. To alleviate concerns about the noise disturbing the horses, Harley-Davidson arranged to have most of the horses in residence at the track re-stabled at nearby Laurel Racetrack. To accommodate those that remained, no activity took place at the site until after every horse had completed its morning workout session.

 **Los Angeles**

California Motor Speedway

September 6–8, 2002

Los Angeles was the next stop on The Open Road Tour, and the California Motor Speedway was the largest of the sites selected. Measuring a mile from one end to the other, its geographical location provided an amazing backdrop for the festivities.

 **Toronto**

Molson Park

September 28–29, 2002

Molson Park in nearby Barrie served as the site when The Open Road Tour visited Canada. A popular location for music festivals, the park-like setting greeted riders with the first signs of fall, with cool temperatures and the first rainy days of the tour.

⭐ Dallas / Fort Worth

Texas Motor Speedway

October 26–27, 2002

The Texas Motor Speedway was the site of the Dallas / Fort Worth tour stop, and while it was cold and damp, the weather didn't keep thousands of riders from attending. As an added challenge, a rock shelf beneath the grounds was discovered during the set up, and it ultimately prevented the Machine tent from being raised.

HARLEY-DAVIDSON
IN THE MOVIES

BIKER STYLE

 ## Sydney

Sydney Olympic Park

March 14–16, 2003

The second leg of the tour took it outside of North America, and the first stop was Sydney Olympic Park in Australia. Originally built for the 2000 Olympics, the site provided virtually new facilities. In addition to being the first time all of the exhibits moved indoors under one roof, the event was noted for the large number of families that attended.

 # Tokyo

Messe Akishima

April 26–27, 2003

The Tokyo event was held at Messe Akishima, 40 miles from downtown Tokyo. The event was held indoors with one large hall housing all of the exhibits. Just to keep the adrenaline going, customs papers were misplaced resulting in the exhibits being held in quarantine until the last possible moment. Nonetheless, the preparations were completed in time for opening ceremonies.

⭐ **8** **Barcelona**

Palau Sant Jordi

June 27–29, 2003

Located on a hill overlooking the city, Barcelona Palau Sant Jordi served as the location for The Open Road Tour. Designed by renowned architect Arako Isosaki, the structure was originally built for the 1982 Olympic Games. Together with the Telefonica Tower by Santiago Calatrava, it made the Barcelona venue one of the most picturesque. Held in conjunction with the European H.O.G.® rally, Barcelona attracted riders from throughout Europe, making it a multi-national event.

★ 9 Hamburg

Harbor Pier 27

July 25–27, 2003

The Hamburg Open Road Tour event was held on Pier 27 in the harbor and had a true festival atmosphere. The unique urban setting for this stop in the heart of Europe allowed visitors to roam the harbor and take in the music and Open Road Tour exhibits at their own pace. The last stop on the tour before it turned back to Milwaukee, the event boasted the largest number of attendees.

THE HARLEY-DAVIDSON
EXPERIENCE

It was everything you could have imagined. And more.

The Harley-Davidson Experience was organized around four m
hemes: Journey: 100 Years of Harley-Davidson; Machine: Th
Motorcycle and the Engine; Culture: Harley-Davidson in the Wo
nd Ride: Harley-Davidson and Buell Today.

Entering each of the 20,000 square foot tents, visitors were
mmersed in a unique environment containing more never-se
before Harley-Davidson artifacts and exhibits than at any oth
ime in the Company's history.

JOURNEY

100 Years of Harley-Davidson

The Shed

A reproduction of the original shed erected in the Davidson family backyard served as a backdrop for an historical film montage that told the story of the Motor Company through stills and moving footage.

100 Years of Harley-Davidson

This exhibit followed the chronology of the Motor Company's history, highlighting major moments and key events that often echoed Harley-Davidson's participation in broader historical events in America. The exhibit wrapped around the perimeter of the tent, turning the walls of the structure into an enormous panorama of Harley-Davidson history. The Company's 100 years were broken down into eras of history and each section showcased a significant motorcycle from that era.

Rider Gallery

The photographs in this exhibit featured Harley-Davidson enthusiasts over the past 100 years. Depicted were riders from all different backgrounds with a shared, enduring passion for riding Harley-Davidson® motorcycles.

↑ Willie G. at 95th anniversary, 199[?]

Davidson Connection

This exhibit gave visitors an opportunity to speak with Willie G. Davidson, Senior Vice-President and Chief Styling Officer, his wife Nancy Davidson and Bill Davidson, Director, Marketing Motorcycle Development. The phone rang at random times and visitors got a chance to ask Willie or the other members of the Davidson family whatever they wanted to know about Harley-Davidson.

MACHINE

The Motorcycle and the Engine

The Archives Collection

This exhibit featured over 30 bikes from the Motor Company's Archives collection. Including civilian, military, police, and racing landmarks, the motorcycles are some of the most significant made by Harley-Davidson over the years.

Manufacturing

This exhibit was an ode to the manufacturing plants and processes of Harley-Davidson as well as their employees in the five manufacturing facilities: Tomahawk Operations, Tomahawk, Wisconsin; Vehicle Operations, York, Pennsylvania; Powertrain Operations, Capitol Drive, Wauwatosa, Wisconsin;

Powertrain Operations, Menomonee Falls, Wisconsin; and Vehicle and Powertrain Operations, Kansas City, Missouri. Vintage photographs of factories and motorcycle parts in different stages of production with time-lapse videos of each plant were displayed.

Tank Graphics

This exhibit featured 100 fuel tanks selected by Willie G. and his fellow designers as their favorites. The unique and distinctive graphic designs and colors used by Harley-Davidson over the years were displayed in a huge tented structure reminiscent of an oversized fuel tank.

CULTURE

Harley-Davidson in the World

Rock & Roll

Created in collaboration with the Rock and Roll Hall of Fame and Museum, this exhibition focused on music and motorcycle culture. Among the artists featured were Elvis Presley, Aerosmith, Alice Cooper, Joan Jett, Lou Reed, John Mellencamp, the Doobie Brothers, ZZ Top, the Allman Brothers, the Eagles, Grand Funk Railroad and U2. Photographs, video clips, guitars, stage outfits, motorcycle clothes, and motorcycles were included.

Biker Style

This retrospective provided highlights from 100 years of motorcycle fashion. Visitors were invited to try-on reproductions of vintage fashions and featured styles included examples of clothing from the early 1900s to the present. Visitors were also able to "try-on" new motorcycles outfitted with a multitude of Genuine Motor Parts and Accessories.

Tattoo

This exhibition featured photographs of tattoo art by some of the most well-known photographers working today. Removable Harley-Davidson® tattoos were also distributed in this area.

RIDE
Harley-Davidson and Buell Today

Here visitors had an opportunity to check out the new Harley-Davidson® and Buell® motorcycles. Motor Company representatives were available to answer any questions visitors had about bikes and all other things Harley. Harley-Davidson® Genuine MotorClothes™ apparel and collectibles, fully customized motorcycles loaded with Genuine Harley-Davidson® Motor Parts and Accessories, and the complete Buell® Motorcycle model line were also featured in this tent.

MUSCULAR DYSTROPHY ASSOCIATION

The 100th Anniversary marked the 23rd year that Harley-Davidson has been associated with the Muscular Dystrophy Association, and once again riders, dealers, employees and suppliers rolled up their sleeves and went to work.

With an ambitious goal of raising $5 million during the 100th Anniversary, it wasn't long before the fundraising activities were underway. The efforts included rider pledges, dealer fundraisers, motorcycle raffles, and pin sales.

By the time the celebration peaked in Milwaukee, the effort had raised more than $7.2 million. Motor Company President and Chief Operating Officer Jim McCaslin presented a check to MDA during the 100th Anniversary Party on Sunday, August 31, 2003.

Supporting the Muscular Dystrophy Association

At each of The Open Road Tour stops throughout the U.S. and the rest of the world, Harley-Davidson highlighted its 23-year relationship with the Muscular Dystrophy Association in a number of ways. The local MDA ambassadors were invited to take to the stage with company executives each evening to talk with the riders about their generosity in helping to find a cure for neuromuscular diseases. In addition, at each location there were fundraising activities, including the sale of event-specific commemorative pins and rockers. The proceeds of those efforts stayed in the communities in which they were raised.

Aerosmith in Dalla, Texas

MUSICAL
PERFORMANCES

It wouldn't be a Harley-Davidson celebration without music, and the 100th Anniversary Open Road Tour lived up to the tradition.

With both national and regional acts performing at every site, the festivals became a non-stop experience with two stages going continuously.

At the United States stops, each night saw top names taking center stage. In Atlanta, the performers included Tim McGraw, Travis Tritt, the Warren Brothers, Indigenous and Journey. The Whalers, Ted Nugent, Hootie and the Blowfish, Billy Idol, and Bob Dylan headlined the Baltimore event.

In Los Angeles, The Doors of the 21st Century, Kid Rock, Stone Temple Pilots, Billy Idol, Earl Scruggs, Nickelback, and the Doobie Brothers performed. While Dallas/Fort Worth performers included Aerosmith, Stone Temple Pilots, the Doobie Brothers and Better than Ezra.

And the momentum kept going as The Open Road Tour left the United States and went international. In Toronto, performers included Kim Mitchell, Bif Naked, David Usher and the The Doors of the 21st Century, who repeated their Los Angeles reunion. INXS headlined in Sydney, along with local talents Jimmy Barnes, Yothu Yindi and Killing Heidi.

The Pretenders and Simple Minds performed in Barcelona in addition to many local Spanish artists. In Hamburg, a music festival took place surrounding the Harley-Davidson exhibits and rider activities, including numerous bands over the three-day event.

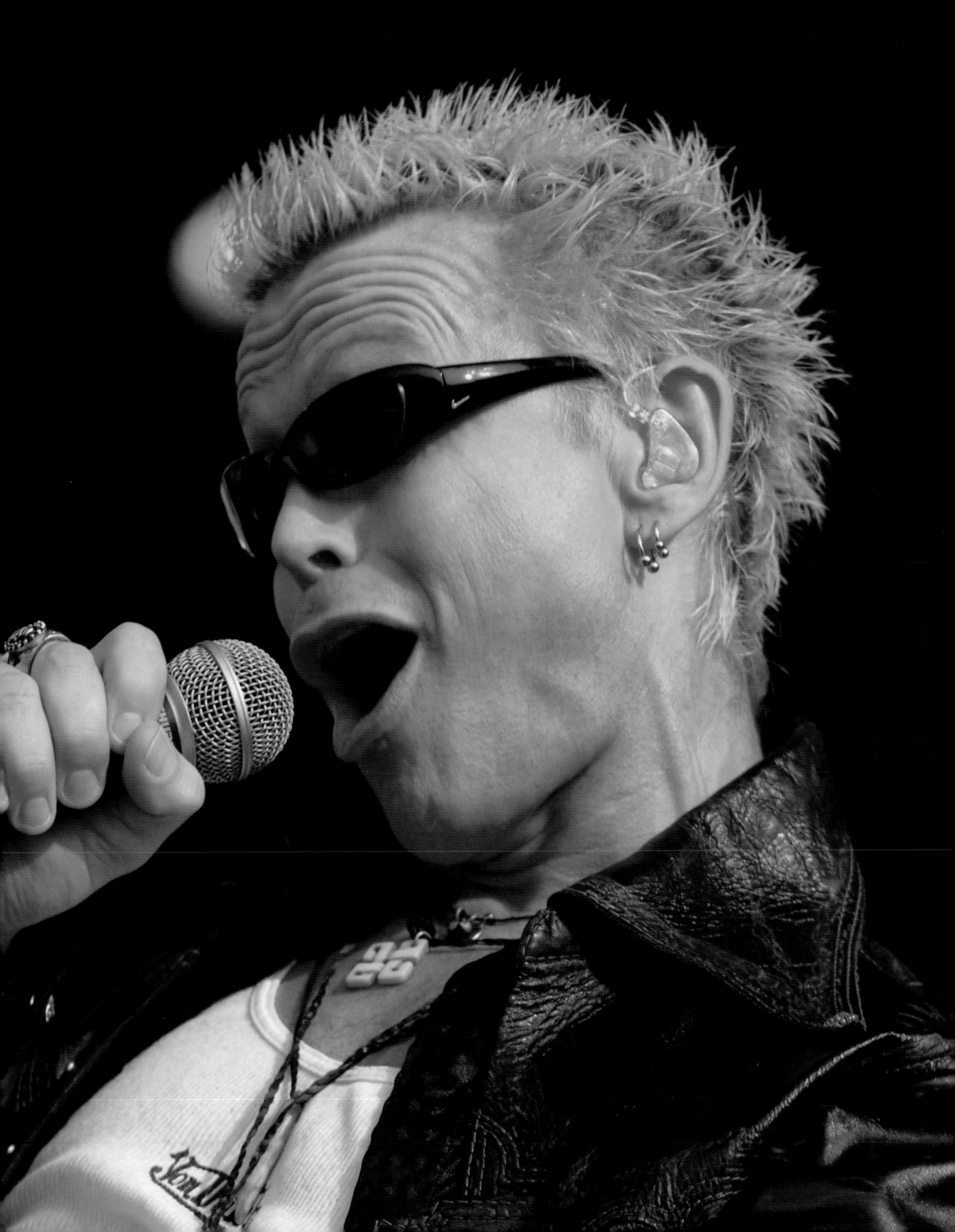

Billy Idol in Baltimore, Maryland

Allison Krauss & Union Station in Atlanta, Georgia

Hootie and the Blowfish in Baltimore, Maryland

Aaron Neville with the Neville Brothers in Baltimore, Maryland

Kid Rock in Los Angeles, California

Default in Los Angeles, California

Robert Cray in Baltimore, Maryland

INXS in Sydney, Australia

Nickelback in Los Angeles, California

Tim McGraw in Atlanta, Georgia

Travis Tritt in Atlanta, Georgia

Lynyrd Skynyrd in Baltimore, Maryland

Seattle Cossacks in Los Angeles

STUNT AND DRILL

They saw it here first.

Sometimes you just want to see what a bike and rider can do, and the Open Road Tour Stunt and Drill teams didn't disappoint.

There was Craig Jones and his sidekick Wing putting on a head-turning, tire burning, helmet scraping stunt show on a Buell® Lightning® XB12F motorcycle. And where they left off, Bubba Blackwell took over with an equally amazing display of stunts performed on his Buell Lightning XB12F and a Buell Blast®.

Not to be outdone, the Marion County Sheriff's Precision Motorcycle Drill Squad and the Seattle Cossacks Motorcycle Stunt and Drill Team cranked things up and delivered memorable performances.

And then there were the drag bikes.

Not just a couple of drag bikes, a lot of drag bikes. The ear splitting, nitro burning demonstrations made for quite an experience.

Performers included Joe Timmons, AHDRA Top Fuel rider and owner of Intermountain Harley-Davidson in Utah; Travis Lummus of the Gene Lummus Harley-Davidson Racing Team, and Ray Price, the 65 year-old legend and racing sensation and owner of Ray Price Harley-Davidson Buell and the Legends of Harley Drag Racing Museum in Raleigh, NC.

Together they smoked the tires and lit up the crowd.

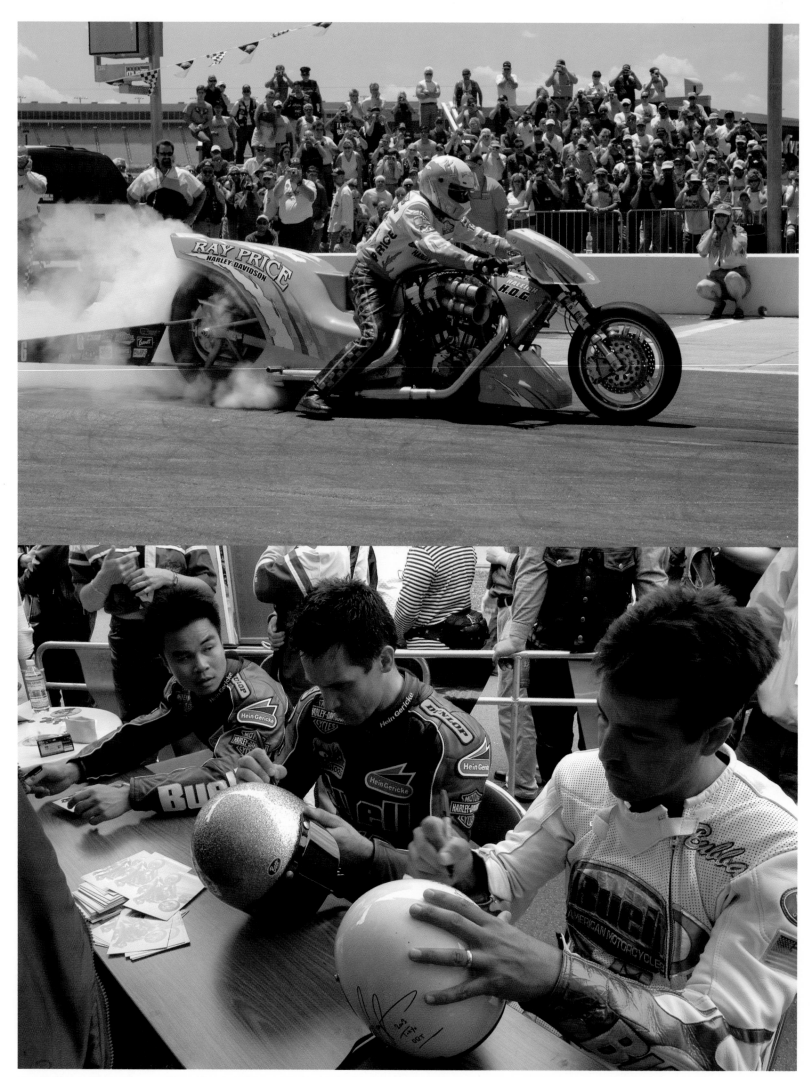

Top: Ray Price in Atlanta, Georgia   Above: Wing, Craig Jones, and Bubba Blackwell in Tokyo, Japan

Bubba Blackwell in Los Angeles, California

Craig Jones in Milwaukee, Wisconsin

Top: Craig Jones in Barcelona, Spain   Above: Craig Jones and Wing in Tokyo, Japan

THE RIDE HOME

If there are moments in life that are destined to seem larger when
a person looks back on them, The Ride Home will be one of them.
For the riders who participated, it was an unforgettable experience.

Starting from Baton Rouge, Louisiana; Las Vegas, Nevada; Portland,
Oregon; and Washington, D.C., the rides made their way across
the country, picking up more riders along the way, and eventually
ended up in Milwaukee for the final four days of the 100th
Anniversary Celebration.

The participants rode with Willie G. Davidson, Jeff Bleustein,
Jim McCaslin, and other Harley-Davidson executives. They took in
street parties and dealer parties at every overnight stop. And
they saw America from the best vantage point one can have — from
the seat of a Harley-Davidson® motorcycle.

The Ride Home Routes

Northeast Route

Washington D.C. to Milwaukee

1,185 miles

Washington D.C., August 21

South Central Route

Baton Rouge, Louisiana to Milwaukee

1,320 miles

Baton Rouge, August 21

Southwest Route

Las Vegas, Nevada to Milwaukee

2,175 miles

Las Vegas, August 18

Northwest Route

Portland, Oregon to Milwaukee

2,225 miles

Portland, August 18

4
3 Buffalo, New York
Dearborn, Michigan
5 Michigan City, Indiana
Harrisburg, Pennsylvania 2
4 Indianapolis, Indiana
Washington, D.C. 1
3 Nashville, Tennessee
mphis, Tennessee

Northeast Route

Washington D.C. to Milwaukee

1,185 miles

Washington D.C., August 21   Washington D.C., August 21

South Central Route

Baton Rouge, Louisiana to Milwaukee

1,320 miles

Baton Rouge, August 21   Baton Rouge, August 21

Southwest Route

Las Vegas, Nevada to Milwaukee

2,175 miles

Las Vegas, August 18   Las Vegas, August 18

Northwest Route

Portland, Oregon to Milwaukee

2,225 miles

Kennewick, August 19   Missoula, August 20

Washington D.C., August 21   Washington D.C., August 21   Washington D.C., August 21

Baton Rouge, August 21   Memphis, August 22   Nashville, August 23

Las Vegas, August 18   Albuquerque, August 20   Albuquerque, August 21

Missoula, August 20   Missoula, August 20   Great Falls, August 21

Washington D.C., August 21   York, August 22   Harrisburg, August 22

Nashville, August 23   Nashville, August 23   Nashville, August 23

Amarillo, August 22   Amarillo, August 22   Amarillo, August 22

Great Falls, August 21   Great Falls, August 21   Great Falls, August 21

Buffalo, August 23

Buffalo, August 24

Michigan City, August 26

Indianapolis, August 24

Indianapolis, August 24

Rockford, August 26

Amarillo, August 22

Amarillo, August 22

Oklahoma City, August 23

Great Falls, August 21

Sturgis, August 23

Sturgis, August 23

Michigan City, August 26

Michigan City, August 26

Milwaukee, August 27

Rockford, August 26

Rockford, August 26

Milwaukee, August 27

Kansas, August 24

Kansas City, August 24

Milwaukee, August 27

Sturgis, August 23

Sturgis, August 24

Milwaukee, August 27

THE
CELEBRATION

When the first of the riders entered the city on August 27th, 2003, you could sense that Milwaukee was ready. It seemed the entire city had turned out. And for the hundreds of thousands of people that got involved for the next three days, the Celebration was almost beyond description.

Following the initial ceremonial countdown at Juneau Avenue, the festivities were non-stop. There were motorcycle demonstration rides, stunt riders, drill teams, and custom and antique bike shows.

There was music at Summerfest, as performances by the likes of Poison, Peter Frampton, Steppenwolf, Billy Idol and Kansas rocked all day and into the night. And at Washington County Fair Park, the Harley Owners Group™ celebrated with Club H.O.G.™ XX, their own 20th anniversary, with performances by B.B. King, Jeff Beck and others.

Meanwhile, at the Milwaukee Art Museum, a special exhibition showcasing Harley-Davidson™ motorcycle design debuted. Rolling Sculptures: The Art of Harley-Davidson attracted more visitors than any other exhibition in the museum's history.

Finally, The Experience site on the shore of the lakefront served as home for all of The Open Road Tour exhibits, the Ford Motor Company display, the Miller Roadside Cafe, and a stage which was the setting for more music and entertainment.

Ceremonial Countdown

On Thursday, August 28, 2003 at 9:00 a.m. the official kick-off for The Celebration was held at 3700 West Juneau Avenue, Harley-Davidson's corporate headquarters, with speeches, fireworks and seemingly endless amounts of confetti.

Summerfest Grounds

The Henry W. Maier Festival Park hosted the Harley-Davidson Workforce exhibit, the Antique and Custom Bike show, and eight stages presented musical and featured entertainment all day long. In addition to top musical acts, other entertainment included stunt and drill teams featuring Craig Jones, Tommy Avala, Team Extreme FMX, and the Marion County Precision Police Drill Team. Chef Biker Billy cooked up some of his favorite dishes—and entertainment for children was featured throughout the day.

Club H.O.G.® XX

2003 also marked the 20th Anniversary of the Harley Owners Group. To celebrate the 750,000-member-strong Harley Owners Group, H.O.G. hosted its own event, Club H.O.G.® XX, at Washington County Fair Park, just north of Milwaukee. The four-day event gave more than 100,000 H.O.G. members from around the world an opportunity to visit with old friends and meet some new ones. Entertainment included B.B. King, Kenny Wayne Shepherd, The Fabulous Thunderbirds and Jeff Beck.

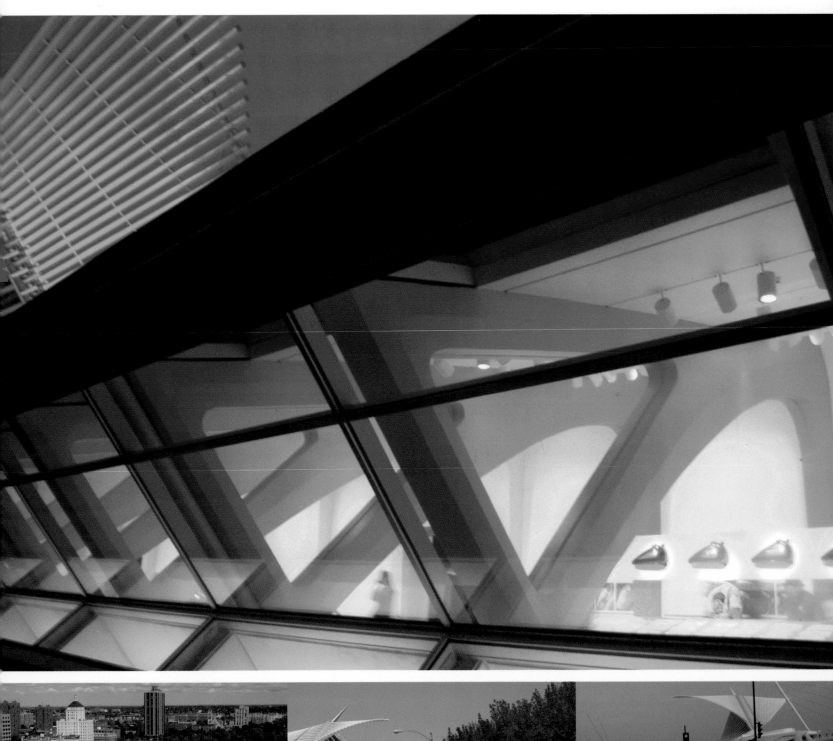

Milwaukee Art Museum

Harley-Davidson® motorcycles are often referred to as rolling sculptures, their design a marriage of engineering, manufacturing and styling creating a fully integrated and functional machine. During Harley-Davidson's 100 year history there have been many styling achievements and milestones. This exhibition explored some of these exemplary designs and illustrated how the Company's heritage and tradition were reflected in its current motorcycles.

Rolling Sculpture
THE ART OF
HARLEY-DAVIDSON

The Experience

Along Lake Michigan enthusiasts reveled in the Harley-Davidson Experience, which featured the four tents that toured the world during The Open Road Tour—Journey, Culture, Machine and Ride. The exhibits immersed enthusiasts in the Harley-Davidson history and lifestyle and gave vistors an opportunity to try the 2004 Harley-Davidson® and Buell® motorcycles on for size.

THE PARADE

Every full-fledged celebration has one.

Yet, as the participants started assembling at the Milwaukee County Zoo, there were indications that this was not going to be an ordinary parade. Maybe it was the look of anticipation in the eyes of the riders that indicated something special was about to happen. Or maybe it was something more obvious.

Like 10,000 bikes.

Out in front — the Parade of MDA Heroes. Those Harley-Davidson riders who had successfully raised $5,300 or more for the Muscular Dystrophy Association.

In three hours that would surely become a part of Harley-Davidson lore, thousands looked on as an endless sea of motorcycles traveled down to the Henry W. Maier Festival Park in an unprecedented display of family pride.

THE PARTY

In the three-week period leading up to The Party, Veteran's Park was transformed into the largest concert venue Milwaukee had ever seen. And as the 150,000 people began arriving, it became clear that the evening was going to be as much about kicking-off the next hundred years of great motorcycles, as it would be about celebrating the past.

Designed as a tribute to the riders and all of the 100th Anniversary participants, the event included an incredible light show and presentations by Harley-Davidson executives including Jeff Bleustein, Jim McCaslin and Willie G. Davidson. Things started warming up with the pre-show featuring highlights from The Open Road Tour, and segments on Harley-Davidson's history and culture.

Then, as host Dan Akroyd took the stage, the night went full throttle.

First, it was the Doobie Brothers performing with the Milwaukee Symphony. Then came performances by Tim McGraw, Kid Rock and Elton John — followed by a spectacular fireworks display that lit up the sky over Lake Michigan.

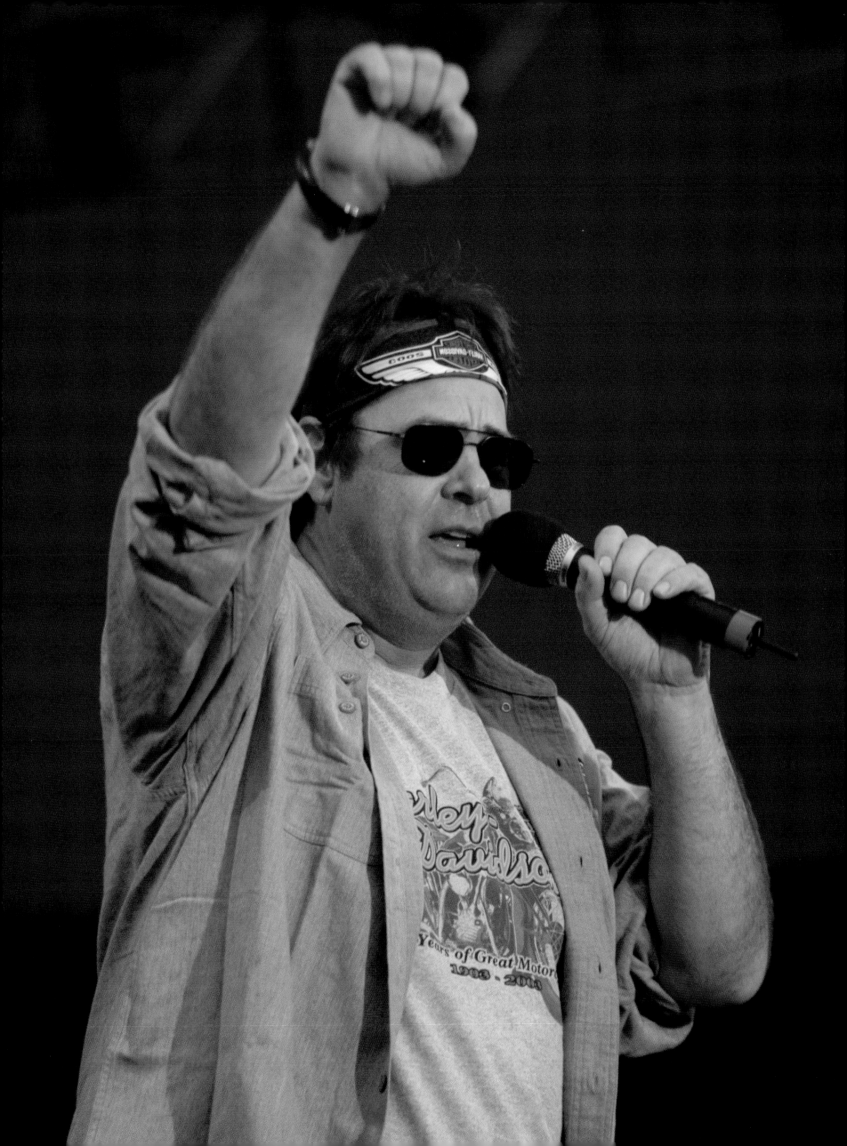

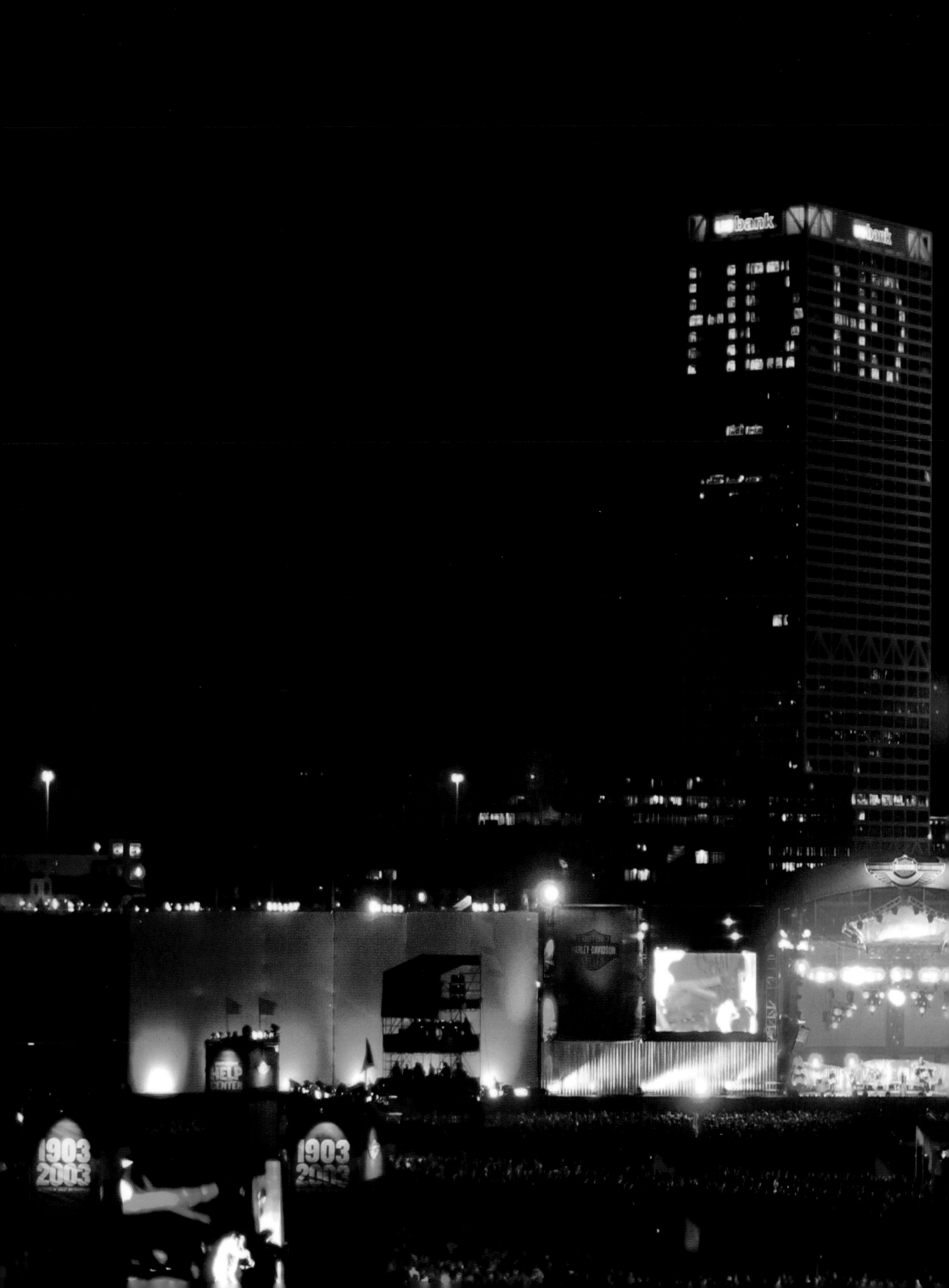

usbank
HD
HELP CENTER
HARLEY-DAVIDSON
1903
2003
1903
2003

Harley-Davidson Motor Company

Harley-Davidson Motor Company
3700 W. Juneau Ave., P.O. Box 653
Milwaukee, Wisconsin 53201
www.harley-davidson.com